Other Life Press Publications:
Bloom Where You Are Transplanted
Eve's Fruit
Our Golden Thread
The Mothers of Jesus: From Matthew's Genealogy
*Thorns to Velvet: Devotional from a Lifetime of Christian
        Experience*

Other Grandmother Earth Publications:
Ashes to Oak
Grandmother Earth I
Grandmother Earth II
Grandmother Earth III
Grandmother Earth IV
Grandmother Earth V
Kinship
My Recollections of Cherokee, Alabama
Of Butterflies and Unicorns
Take Time to Laugh: It's the Music of the Soul
The Southern Railway: From Stevenson to Memphis
*To Love a Whale: Learning about Endangered Animals from
        the Young at Heart*
View from a Mississippi River Cotton Sack

Cover design by Frances Cowden and Dax Jones

Cover photo is Ryan Allen Brinkley, son of Charles
Brinkley, and grandson of Frances Brinkley Cowden

ANGELS: MESSENGERS OF LOVE AND GRACE

Drawing by Madeline Colleen Brinkley, Age 7

ANGELS: MESSENGERS OF LOVE AND GRACE

Frances Brinkley Cowden
Editor

Martha McNatt
Contributing Editor

Frances Darby
Editorial Assistant

Illustrations
by
Madeline Colleen Brinkley
and
Nikolas Bogdanovic Brinkley

The stories in this book are based on
true experiences.

Life Press
Memphis, Tennessee

Library of Congress Cataloging-in-Publication Data

Angels : messengers of love and grace / Frances Brinkley Cowden,
    editor ; Martha McNatt, contributing editor ; Frances Darby,
    editorial assistant ; illustrations by Madeline Colleen Brinkley and
    Nikolas Bogdanovic Brinkley. -- lst ed.
        p. cm.
    ISBN 1-884289-18-5 (pbk.)
        1. Angels. 2. Miracles.   I. Cowden, Frances Brinkley.
II. McNatt, Martha. III. Darby, Frances, 1925- .
BL477.A536 1999
235' .3--dc2l   98-44568
                                                                CIP

ISBN 1-884289-18-5 9.95

FIRST EDITION: 1999
Life Press
P. O. Box 241986
Memphis, Tennessee 38124

CONTENTS

•§§•

ACKNOWLEDGEMENTS

A special thanks for editorial assistance from:

Lorraine Smith
Patricia W. Smith
Dr. Rosemary Stephens
Dr. Malra Treece
Marcelle Brinkley Zarshenas

...and for all of the prayers from friends for
guidance in the production of this book.

Praise him, all his angels,
praise him, all his heavenly hosts.
Psalms 148:2 (NIV)

MESSENGERS OF LOVE

On wings of love they come
to soothe our earthly pain.
Even if we are not aware
of how they've stopped the rain,
they leave bits of heaven
sewn with our souls
to cherish and to share.

--Frances Brinkley Cowden

Drawing by Madeline Colleen Brinkley, Age 7

INTRODUCTION:
ANGELS IN OUR TIME

"I need an angel," he said in much the same manner he would have asked me for a pencil or sheet of paper in the third grade. But this was not the third grade --it was the adult Willis, and it was at our 41st-year high school reunion. Willis Forrester is probably one of the most conservative people I have known--straightforward in the Southern Baptist tradition.

Although his life has been far from ordinary, Willis is down-to-earth and enjoys the same things most other people do. He has his grandson's picture on his Web page.

Angel stories, once reserved for fantasy or direct quotations from the Bible, are becoming more and more a part of the reality of our lives. The angel stories in this book vary from the certainty of seeing, touching or hearing an angel to questions. Was it an angel? Could it have been anything else? All have one thing in common, the belief that the angel or angels brought a message of God's love to each individual's life.

Will Willis get his angel? I do believe that if one has an urgent need for a messenger from God, and if he prays believing or even if he does not pray, a guardian angel might be there. Each of us may have an angel near and not be aware of it. As Christians we believe that angels are never to be prayed to and it is God's decision and not ours as to whether God will choose to send an angel to our aid.

Not everyone who has an angel experience prays for it. Like the grace of God, angels seem to appear to

3

even the least likely people and at the most unlikely times. Sometimes we are not quite certain whether our benefactor is really an angel or a human being sent by God.

When I was telling an acquaintance how an angel saved my son's life in a triple blow-out on his tool-laden van, she said simply, "No angel saved my brother. He was killed instantly."

Why do angels intervene in some instances and not in others? The purpose of this book is to glorify God and not man. Those who have received what they consider to be angel experiences are no more worthy than those who have not. We know that Christ most often ministered to the least likely people. It is with humility and gratitude that we share our stories.

> *Do not let anyone who delights in false humility and the worship of angels disqualify you for the prize. Such a person goes into great detail about what he has seen, and his unspiritual mind puffs him up with idle notions.* Colossians 2:18 (NIV)

Why do angels appear after a tragedy--death of a loved one, rape, etc.--instead of before? Wouldn't you think God would have sent the angel to stop the tragedy rather than to wait and help deal with the aftermath?

Do angels sometimes defy laws of nature? Do they save us in supernatural ways because we have not yet fulfilled God's plan for us?

Do angels escort us home when it is time for us to leave this world? This seems to be a common belief which has no conflict with scripture. Does the dark angel also claim his own at the time of death?

Do our loved ones die and become angels? This concept has been expressed in literature, especially in the Victorian era, but I have found no Biblical support for this theory. Two of our stories are about the mother or grandmother of the writer returning as an angel to give them messages of love and encouragement.

I turned down several stories about loved ones coming back as angels; I did not want any semblance of the New Age view of angels, but one writer convinced me that God could send an angel in any form He wished.

The Holy Spirit speaks within us, but angels are an outward manifestation of God's love. Do they speak within us also? Perhaps it was the Holy Spirit that spoke within one writer, but it was the physical appearance of an angel that got her attention even though the angel turned out to be balloons. See "A Message from an Angel."

References to angels in the Bible are myriad. The same is true of the way angels have captured the imagination of man in his art and in his literature. Many books about angels have been resplendent with art from the masters, but I chose to have young children illustrate this book. The children were of course influenced by classical portrayals of angels, but they brought their own innocence to the subject.

This book could raise more questions than it answers. Angels are a part of the heavenly plan--their reason for being is to glorify God but a part of their day-to-day mission is described in Hebrews 1:14, "Are not all angels ministering spirits sent to serve those who will inherit salvation." The specifics of how and why they work is one of God's mysteries we do not understand.

We do hope that you will be blessed by the experiences we are sharing.

Frances Brinkley Cowden
Editor

5

Drawing by Nikolas Bogdanovic Brinkley, Age 8

TO WATCH OVER ME

For he will command his angels concerning you to guard you in all your ways; they will lift you up in their hands, so that you will not strike your foot against a stone.

Psalms 91: 11-12 (NIV)

Drawing by Nikolas Bogdanovic Brinkley, Age 8

THE UNSEEN HAND

Frances Brinkley Cowden

I do not know why the touch frightened me, except that I was six years old. I was sleeping near the wall. Normally when I was at my grandma's house, I slept with my teen-age aunt, Molly; but she had spent the night with a friend. I don't remember anything else except that I refused to sleep near the wall for many years to come no matter where I was.

About 13 years later when I was awakened by that touch again, it was an entirely different matter. This time I felt myself being pushed back over on my side to a 90 degree angle with the bed. I was right on the edge of my grandmother's bed and had been about to roll over and off the high bed onto the floor. My husband was sleeping against me and I had no space left for turning over as I inevitably do in my sleep.

At the time I was six months pregnant with my first child. I have no doubt that had I hit the floor on my back, my life and the life of my child would have been in jeopardy. There may have never been other children. I remember the gentle shove until this day. My son, Guy Jr., will be 40 this year.

I felt the hand once more just recently when I was sleeping in a bed other than my own and was about to fall off the bed again. A drawer of the night stand was open. If I had fallen, I would have hit my head at the very least.

My husband also had an occasion to feel the touch of that hand. He had a habit of being awakened in the middle of the night by some noise. He would jump up, wake me and grab his gun from the shelf above the television. He would creep through the house to look out

9

of the front and back doors while I lay in bed waiting for him to return and say that it was nothing.

But one night it was different. He awakened with a certainty that he had heard someone. This time I was convinced we really had an intruder. I picked up the portable phone ready to dial 911-Emergency, and said a prayer that no one would be hurt. I didn't want my husband to shoot someone and I didn't want him to be shot.

I followed him by a couple of minutes and went into the dark den while he was looking out the front door. He was on the way back to the bedroom having made his rounds, and I was coming back into the hall behind him. He heard me, turned around, and fired the gun at me at very close range.

I screamed as I saw the flash and felt the heat of the bullet that went past my face and into the wall behind me. Realizing what he had done, he turned on the light.

He said he felt a hand hit his hand just as he fired, deflecting his aim. The hand of my guardian angel had saved me once more! After that night the gun was put away where no one could get it so easily. Ever since then he has trusted our security alarm. And I--I pray each night as I lie down to sleep.

ANGELS HAVE HUGE WINGS

Gayle Fleming Hulsey

In my work as a realtor, I travel the roads every day across Memphis and Shelby County. I truly believe the Interstate Highway 240 Loop, Memphis, Tennessee, is watched by angels. They save lives, and perhaps have a "death watch" for those who do not survive.

There is one particular place about two-and-a-half to three miles along 1-240 South Side. This part of the interstate and the roads that feed into it seems to be especially dangerous. I have had two minor accidents there myself. This is basically a "tough" area with heavy industry. Perhaps the frustration of those who live there contributes to this dangerous situation. I have seen terrible accidents, even death more than once.

One hot summer day I was on an errand around the I-240 Loop when suddenly, in front of me, a black pick up truck flipped up and over. It had struck something just ahead of it. At sixty miles per hour--no time--no way could I brake in time to avoid the deadly pile up. So I prayed for guidance for myself and all the souls on that road. Strangely enough, I felt compelled not to touch the brakes. My car began to float with my hand gently steering it to the left across two busy, fast lanes of traffic. It then rolled softly onto the shoulder. I stopped about three hundred feet in front of the accident. I was puzzled after I regained my composure; I had not a scratch.

I concluded that God's messengers were sent to save my life. Apparently, huge unseen wings folded around my car and gently floated it across the highway to safety. My gratitude is everlasting. I thank God for my life and that angels have huge wings.

11

NO EXIT

Frances Darby

I was not overly excited about the trip to Pigeon Forge and Gatlinburg, the Garden of Eden of the Smokies, in East Tennessee. It was a long drive from Memphis to attend a business meeting, but I was hoping the doctor who was speaking could tell me something to help my ailing husband.

At that time Jim had not yet been diagnosed with Parkinson's Disease, and we were reaching out in all directions to find what we could do to relieve the anger that was mounting from the frustration of not knowing what was happening.

This was a part-time business as I was already employed full-time. The coordinator, another supervisor and I left Memphis early in the morning. It was such a relief to finally arrive at the Holiday Inn and get settled in.

It was so crowded at the meeting we had to stand at the back of the room and wait for the question-and-answer period. My questions were not answered to my satisfaction because more information was necessary than I had available.

The next morning we got a late start home. Rain began to fall early in the trip. Driving became taxing for the coordinator, so I agreed to take the wheel. She got into the back seat and was soon asleep.

The sky darkened and driving along the mountainous highway was not pleasant. I could not look around to see the homes of the stars while going through

12

Nashville. Night driving was even more treacherous because of the glare from the lights and the wet pavement.

I don't know what happened. Perhaps I became sleepy, closed my eyes to rest or was blinded by rain-splattered headlights. But I found I had begun to take an exit on a steep incline. When I realized my error, I felt a sense of the car going down the mountain and everything was black--the three of us hurtling through space. At this point I had a vague feeling of unconcern.

The other supervisor was in the passenger seat and she yelled. "You are not supposed to get off the highway here!"

I slammed on the brakes and felt a sense of the car floating in space. When we stopped, the car was facing down the ramp back toward the highway. Another car was behind us and stopped to avoid hitting us or to see if we were all right.

The coordinator was thrown from the back seat. Her knee hit the forward seat, but she said in a sleepy daze. "Are we all right?"

I don't know if angels were responsible for the car making the one hundred-eighty-degree turn, but we could not think of any other explanation. Thanking God, I managed to get back on the highway and drove the rest of the journey home. I don't remember being too frightened during the episode, and I believe there was a divine purpose in our being saved.

✓

13

OUR ANGELIC ARTISAN

Valerie Esker

Next February, Jim and I will celebrate our thirty-ninth wedding anniversary. "How nice," you say, mentally noting that even in this day of disposable marriages, this doesn't merit any special awards. You're right! Many older couples have topped that milestone, by decades. However, our romance was touched by an unseen benefactor: a benefactor who, it seems, helped sculpt our shared destiny. We feel, that by spiritual design, an angelic encounter was what we had experienced, that night so long ago.

Looking at us now, you would not see us as especially attractive. We wear our years with an average kind of wear and tear. Though we rarely express affection publicly, we clearly enjoy each other's company. We are best friends and lovers, as well as Mom and Dad, Grandma and Grandpa, and recently, great-grandparents! Yet, through the years, there were times when we weren't altogether certain that we would continue to be, a "we!" Our human flaws, youthful shallowness, and the stress of raising a family often cast a shadow over the love-aura that lit our lives in the beginning.

That "beginning" was in summer school. Because we each had failed a math course in our respective schools, we were required to make-up the credit by attending a centrally located school.

14

At fifteen, I was excruciatingly shy, and a bookworm. I excelled academically in English and literature. Math? That was another story! I dreaded the thought of a summer filled with dreary, difficult equations. The day I entered that dreaded classroom, I didn't know what blessings Providence had in store.

Until that fateful summer, I had never dated. My acutely shy nature kept me away from the teen social scene. Though aware of boys, I was not keenly so. But that day, as I walked to my assigned desk with eyes cast downward, I felt that someone was staring at me. Though I hadn't glanced up to meet his gaze, I knew instinctively a newly responsive chord in my soul had been sounded!

I soon discovered that the "someone," was Jim. He was destined to be my one and only soul-mate!

Summer, and our romance, progressed. I managed to pass the class with a "C" grade. In the fall, we returned to our usual schools, on opposite sides of town. Although we were permitted to date only on weekends, puppy love grew serious; so serious, my protective parents had forbidden us further contact. We then met on the sly, but the stolen moments were bittersweet. We suffered an anguish only adolescents can know! A year dragged by slowly.

To assuage our anguish, we pooled our meager resources and hopped a Greyhound bus to Cleveland, sixty miles distant. Once there, we began a lengthy hike, which lasted through the sweltering August afternoon, until nightfall. We were tired, broke, and growing concerned about our fate. Feeling stupid, we knocked on a weathered door in a seedy part of town. A rotund lady with a friendly smile listened sympathetically to our spiel. We claimed we were siblings traveling together, down on our luck. To our amazement, she put us up for the night... in separate rooms!

15

Early next day, we were on our way once more, planning to walk to Detroit, where Jim's uncle lived. He would be our refuge! The distance seemed great, but not impossibly so. We trudged along, leaving the outskirts of Cleveland behind. City sidewalks gave way to rural highways. Trucks sped by, trailing diesel smoke. As they passed, their tires whined plaintively, echoing the mood of our troubled thoughts. Mid-day, we stopped to rest in a field, hungrily devouring two candy bars. Jim's hay fever symptoms worsened. My feet ached. We wondered how we could have forsaken our safe, comfortable homes! The memory of being separated. though, drove us onward, through the steamy afternoon heat and into the night.

About midnight, searching for shelter, we ambled down a side road, away from the headlights. We had entered a small residential area of neat little homes. The late hour precluded any possibility of asking for help. I remember it as an enchanted night. A cricket chorus serenaded us. A blanket of stars was flung across the sky. The night air was cool, but it failed to revive our sinking spirits and tired bodies.

We found ourselves approaching an ornate, gothic-looking church. There were deep, dark alcoves fronting the high doorways ... a safe place to sleep without fear of being discovered! The rough cement proved an uncomfortable bed, but sleep came quickly. A dog barked, far in the distance. Jim cradled my head on his shoulder, and we drifted off.

Suddenly, I was awakened by Jim's voice. I struggled through a heavy fog of sleep, hearing him cry, "What... ?" He was sitting up.

"Who are you talking to?" I mumbled.

"Didn't you call my name?" he asked.

"No, I was sleeping," I yawned.

16

Weariness outweighed any need to ponder the curious incident, and again we slept. Then the strange episode recurred! This time, I heard someone call my name! It wasn't Jim, though. He was clearly sound asleep. Something really weird was going on! Could our extreme state of exhaustion, cause these audible hallucinations? I tried to calm myself, but it all began again.

Spooked, I watched Jim awaken as if in response to a ghostly vocal bidding. We clung together, our eyes wide in the semi-darkness. A presence, a benevolent, sentinel spirit, was with us! It surrounded us with an almost tangible, caring watchfulness. Without spoken words, it conveyed that it was guiding us, protecting us. It assured us that all would end well. We felt ashamed of our bold misadventure, but such loving acceptance emanated from this magnanimous being, we could focus only on that! Mysteriously, we were lulled into a deep, undisturbed slumber.

At daybreak we woke refreshed. A lingering sense of wonder prevailed as we resumed our highway pilgrimage, but in a few hours our trek was abruptly over. Our distraught parents had reported us missing, and an alert patrolman spotted us walking along the highway leading to Michigan. By evening, we were returned to our angry, but relieved, families. Of course, as we had predicted, this Romeo and Juliet were again forbidden any communication with one another.

Our lives temporarily took separate pathways. The difficulty of nurturing a relationship under strong family disapproval was too great. Jim joined the Air Force. At seventeen, I entered into a short-term, unhappy marriage. Still, time couldn't quell our longing to be together, and we joyfully resumed our undeniable love story! At nineteen, we wed, blessed by our parents.

17

When we reminisce about that foolish summer, we still thrill in awe of that unforgettable angel encounter. Recently, I composed a sonnet about our celestial friend. Thanks to him, God's special emissary, all really has ended well!

ANGELS

Do angels ever move within our lives,
When helping fate assume its rightful pose
By intervening with their artful knives,
Then carving out our future's eyes and nose?
Well, hear how my seraphic story goes ...
Long years ago, two lovers ran away.
Quite young they were, still in their parents' care;
Near grown, but really children out to play!
They dwell together to this very day,
Because a voice had whispered to the two,
That God ordained that they should always stay
Together, 'til to Him, someday they flew
Entwined forever, blessed with wedded bliss.
And so it was. An angel sculpted this!

--Valerie Esker

MY ANGEL ?

Louise Stovall Hays

The hospital corridors were hushed. It was the second night of battle against growing problems which had brought me to the Emergency Room. After a series of tests I was admitted to a room well after midnight. The only sounds I could hear were those of the machinery and gadgets hooked to my body. They clicked and hummed at a steady and monotonous pace.

As I lay in bed, nurses came and went. They checked the machinery that registered pulse rate, blood pressure and heart activity. Wires fastened to my chest sent these measurements to a screen monitored down the hall. Nights and days ran together in my agony.

Suddenly I became aware of a faint rustling at my bedside and the soft voice of an "angel." Leaning close, she told me that she was trying to reach my doctor because my heart rate was too rapid. Softly and quietly, with soundless footsteps, she left to attend to the details, which resulted in much hurried activity. Nurses and technicians appeared, bustling around with more needles, more machinery; and, always hovering to supervise the work, was my angel. Her presence was a like a calming aura. When all was in place and the bustling subsided, a peace settled over the room and I slept. One crisis down and one to go.

The next evening a new doctor entered my room and introduced himself as a thoracic surgeon. He said that it would be necessary to perform a painful procedure.

Then, as if from nowhere, the same "angel" whom I had not seen in the past twenty-four hours appeared again.

19

Easily and quietly she approached and said, "I'll be here with you." She tried to make me comfortable and ready for the experience, saying, "I'm going to hold you, don't be afraid." A feeling of tranquillity filled my being. There was no fear, no apprehension, and when it was over my angel just as suddenly disappeared.

I never saw her again, leaving me to wonder if she was real or if I had given her wings made from my gossamer hold on reality.

VOICE ABOVE THE RAGTIME

James Roberson, as told to Martha McNatt

A few years back, we moved into an ancient farmhouse, built before 1800 from logs cut along the Rappahannock River by the Foster family. In later years, the logs had been covered with clapboard, the inside had been updated, and ownership had passed from the original family to Mr. Clare, who lived in town, but kept cattle on the farmland which surrounded the house.

We were attracted to the old house because of the soundproof qualities of the walls which were two feet thick all through the house. My wife, Margaret, is a Conservatory graduate in vocal performance, and I play horns, drums, and piano in my job as a high school band director. The noise level in our home could be annoying to neighbors, and we sometimes annoyed each other as we practiced for performances and worked on lesson plans for students.

In summer, I often enjoyed watching the cows as they grazed in the pastures around the house, but by late summer, weeds grew high and thick around the fence and blocked the visibility of the animals. From time to time, one of the farm workers would come into the fields with a large mowing machine and clear out the tall weeds which obstructed our view.

It was a late summer day. I had hurried home from school to enjoy the coolness of the old house and to seize a few moments alone to practice a Scott Joplin solo

21

for an upcoming performance. As I approached the house, I noticed the man on a mowing machine working in one of the fields behind the house.

I poured a glass of iced tea and settled myself at the Grand to practice. Ragtime music is loud, and I was attacking the solo with all the energy I could muster. After a few minutes, I heard a voice through the living room wall. "Go outside!"

Controlling my irritation, I called out, "Come on in. The door is open," and continued to play. Nobody responded to my invitation. I walked to the window and looked outside. Nobody was there. I went back to the piano, convincing myself the voice had been from somebody passing by the house.

As soon as I began playing, the voice sounded again. "Go outside." This time I cracked the door slightly and peeked outside. Some of my band students delighted in playing jokes on me. I suspected that they were hiding in the bushes, waiting for my reaction.

I resumed my loud practicing. This time the voice was more demanding. I heard it clearly above the loud sounds of my piano. "Go outside." I could not continue to ignore the plea.

I walked into the yard, and I noticed the stillness. The mowing machine which had been cutting near the back fence was silent. In a matter of seconds, I heard a weak voice coming from the direction of the cow pasture. "Help me, please. Somebody help me."

I am not the athletic type, but I cleared the back fence in one leap. Breaking through the weeds, I could see a hand waving to me from the tall grass near the machine. Panting and running, I reached the man who was obviously in great pain. A stick was protruding from a bleeding wound in his leg, which was beginning to swell. I knew he needed professional help. I found his cap and put

22

it over his eyes to protect them from the hot sun and I raced to the house to call the rescue squad.

Within minutes, he was transported to the hospital by ambulance. I was so exhausted I had to go back into the house to regain control of myself. I immediately began to realize what had happened to me. I had heard a voice call me to go outside. I knew that the injured man could not have called out loudly enough for me to hear, and even if he had, he would not have said "Go outside."

When I visited him in the hospital two days later, I felt compelled to ask him whether he had called out to me from the field. "No, I didn't call," he said "I only prayed to God to send someone to help me before I bled to death. It was surely an Angel of the Lord who was calling to you."

I have not heard the angelic voice again, but I am convinced a heavenly being was involved in my opportunity to minister to someone in need on that summer day.

OBSESSION CAST ASIDE

Norma Dennison, as told to Martha McNatt

I have a few strong obsessions concerning my home. The strongest concern is my distaste for dirty dishes in the sink. One Saturday, I was preparing food for the Church Picnic. I looked in the pantry for a can of pineapple, but no pineapple was to be found. "I will make a quick trip to the store," I said aloud, but the sight of a sink full of dishes changed my mind.

"I need to wash the dishes before I go," I reasoned.

I was alone in the house. My husband and our brood of three had walked a few blocks down the street for a visit with his mother. I started washing dishes. "You really need to go to the store now," said a voice inside my head. "But I can't leave the sink full of dishes," said my other self. I washed another pan. The voice became more insistent. "Go to the store--now!" It was almost a command.

I gave in. Leaving the dishes, I drove to the store a mile away. I paid little attention to the fact that the sky had become overcast and a sprinkle of rain was falling on my windshield. While I was in the store, I heard a loud thunderclap and saw a flash of cloud to ground lightning.

I had been away from the house no more than twenty minutes, but as I turned the last comer, I could see that something had happened. Fire trucks were in the yard. People were running toward our house. Smoke was boiling out of the kitchen window.

Firemen were inside. Smoke was thick, but no fire was visible. Lightning had traveled along the outside electric wiring and had entered the house just above my kitchen sink. The sink was now empty. Pots and pans were strewn around the kitchen, and a jagged hole five inches wide was in the bottom of the sink.

The voice inside my head returned. This time it whispered. "God is our refuge and strength, an ever present help in trouble." --Psalm 46:1 (NIV) God's messenger had indeed been present in my kitchen that day. The message broke through my obsession for clean dishes and led me away from the wrath of nature.

A CHANGE IN PLANS

Jane Mayfield, as told to Martha McNatt

We were in a western city best known for conventions and casinos. I was representing my profession at a national meeting, and my husband Van was along for the free-time opportunities for fun and sightseeing. From our hotel window, we could see dozens of tourist traps offering tours, shows, and souvenir merchandise. Being an adventurous pair, we were attracted to the sign that advertised flying trips above the Grand Canyon some sixty miles distant.

We spread the word among our friends that we were interested in making the fly-over, hoping another couple would be willing to join us. We had no takers. Early in our first free afternoon, we told our friends good-bye and walked toward the departure point for the tour. We had seen the canyon from every overlook point, and we both were in awe of its beauty and grandeur. "What a thrill it will to be to see it from the air!" I told Van as we approached our destination.

We were almost to the door when another sign caught my eye. It said that only two seats remained available for a desert tour leaving within fifteen minutes. Something inside of me propelled me toward the ticket counter. Suddenly, I felt a strong attraction to the desert tour instead of the canyon fly-over. Van was appalled with my sudden change of mind, but he yielded to my persuasion. We joined the desert tour at the last minute and boarded the tour van.

The desert tour did not fulfill our expectations. Van grumbled a bit as we bumped and sweated through two hours of sand, dark rock outcroppings, and a mesa with terra-cotta stripes and scrubby vegetation. It was almost dinner time as we walked wearily back to the hotel.

When we entered the lobby, a roar went up from about a dozen of our friends who were gathered around a T.V. set. Several rushed forward to hug us. We were stunned. We had not been greeted so enthusiastically at any other time.

"Thank God, you are alive," said my best friend, tears streaming down her face. The six o'clock news reporter, just moments before, had reported that a small plane flying tourists over the Grand Canyon had crashed, killing everyone aboard. It was the plane that we would have taken for our canyon adventure. God had saved us from sudden death.

I often ponder the eternal question humans ask when God performs an earthly miracle. Why? Why were we warned? All afternoon I had battled with myself concerning my dramatic change of mind. I knew it was more than a sudden whim. I did not know it was a life-saving maneuver. I believe it was the voice of an angelic messenger sent from God.

It was also a life-changing event. Every morning I offer my day to God. Perhaps one day, as I interact with friends, customers and strangers, I will recognize the purpose for which I was saved. My joy is overflowing as each day unfolds.

UPSIDE DOWN MIRACLE

Cheryl Davis, as told to Martha McNatt

*And pray in the Spirit on all occasions with all kinds of
prayers and requests*---Ephesians 6:18 (NIV)

I was almost late for my shift at a manufacturing
plant in the county industrial park, five miles outside the
city. Rain was coming down hard, but I decided to take
the short cut through a rural road, which was narrow but
smooth. I was less than a mile from the plant entrance
when my small car went into a skid, made a ninety degree
turn, and headed down a fifteen foot embankment toward
a water filled creek.

As I went down the embankment I continued to
hold the steering wheel, driving down the steep slope, but
at the bottom, the car hit the creek bank and flipped into
the stream. When my head stopped spinning, the car was
upside down with its hood in the water, but I was right
side up. My body was folded between the two upside
down seats. My feet pushed against the top of the car.

I could hear water seeping in through the front of
the car, and I immediately realized I was in mortal danger
of drowning. I prayed one sentence: "Lord, get me out of
here!" The words were barely out of my mouth when the
back of the back seat fell from its upside down position
and splashed in the water around my feet. As it fell a space
opened before me, large enough for me to crawl through.
I have never been sure whether it was the back window
which, I discovered later, was completely broken out in the
wreckage, or the open trunk.

28

The back of the car was resting on the creek bank, and I was able to climb out onto the slippery embankment. I had started to scramble up toward the road when I heard someone shouting, "Are you all right? Is anybody else in the car?" I was incoherent, but I felt no pain, and my rescuers quickly called for an ambulance. I was scratched and bruised but required only emergency room treatment.

Two miracles are evident to me in this episode. The immediate answer to my prayer convinced me that God had sent an angel to rescue me from certain death. I am convinced my life has a purpose. The second miracle had occurred earlier, but I did not know it. I had failed to fasten my seat belt at the beginning of my journey. I always wear my seat belt fastened. If I had followed my usual pattern that day, I would have been upside down in the car with my head in the seeping water.

If I ever doubted God's awareness of me as an individual, I never will doubt again. If I ever questioned the presence of angels, I will never question again. My faith is strong, my feeling of self worth is confirmed, and my desire to serve Him is constant.

LEFT TURN RIGHT TURN

Jane Isaac, as told to Martha McNatt

I was a Public Health Nurse in a small town in the Great Plains. My job description included visits in homes where children were at risk for abuse, neglect, or poverty. Among my clients was a Hispanic immigrant family with ten children from infancy to age fourteen.

On a summer morning, I had scheduled a visit to the above described home. Nurse visits were always unannounced in order to observe life in its usual state. As I approached the neighborhood, I realized that lunch time was near. I knew that friends from my office would be lunching at the hospital, which was in the same vicinity. I made a quick decision. I would go by the hospital and have lunch with my friends before I made the scheduled home visit.

The hospital was a right turn, and the client's home was a left turn. As I came into the intersection, my mind said right turn, but my car made a left turn. At that moment an unseen force was in charge of my automobile.

Feeling the impact of the experience, I determined that my home visit had to be the priority. I felt a heavenly presence as I went speeding toward the run-down shack on an unpaved street. Turning into the dusty driveway, I could hear loud screaming. I jumped from the car just as the mother came out of the door and yelled at me, "I spilled a pan of grease down my arm. I need a doctor."

30

She needed more than a doctor. Raw flesh of third degree burns was visible on her arm from her elbow to her fingertips.

I pushed her toward my car, snatched three preschoolers off the porch, and headed for the hospital emergency room. Once the mother was receiving care, I drove to the high school and asked permission to take the fourteen-year-old home to manage the brood of little ones. I never got any lunch that day. I spent the afternoon making arrangements for my charges.

Years have passed since the day my car disobeyed my brain. I am convinced it was a heavenly signal conveyed by a messenger from God. Within a few weeks, my client's family disappeared in the middle of the night.

Until this day, the sight of a Hispanic mother with a big brood of children reminds me of them. I always look for a burn-scarred arm.

A CUSHIONED FALL

Martha McNatt

It was the week before Christmas. We were invited to a dinner party in the home of friends from our church. In the same neighborhood lived a couple with whom we always exchanged small gifts at Christmas. Knowing they were leaving town for the holidays, we decided to make a quick stop at their house to deliver gifts, on the way to the party. We stayed for a short visit, and as we were leaving, my friend handed me a package the size of a small shoe box, which she said contained something fragile which I was not to open until Christmas Day.

I was wearing dress flats with a long skirt, which was quite a departure from the Keds and jeans in which I normally live. As I stepped out the door, one smooth soled shoe skidded off the top step and I was headed for the concrete carport four steps below.

I seemed to fall in slow motion. I was aware of the fragile package in my hands, and waiting for the crushing blow I knew was coming. The crash never came. I floated to the concrete, where I landed in an undignified position, but I was totally uninjured. I had a small scrape on my left shoulder which brushed the bottom step. My guardian angel must have been on duty, although I felt no tangible support from hands or wings.

I brushed myself off, and when I had regained my composure we went to the party instead of the hospital. I held in my hands visible proof of the divine presence. My fragile package was completely intact. Not a scratch or a crack on the white china tea pot inside.

MONDAY MORNING ANGEL

Martha McNatt

About midway into her ninetieth year, Velma arose early as she usually did on Monday. She had lived alone for fifteen years following the death of her husband. She prepared her breakfast of oatmeal, toast and juice, and lingered over a cup of coffee and the Sunday newspapers, which she had not finished yesterday. She collected a load of laundry and started her automatic washing machine, then mixed a batch of sugar cookies for the Women's Meeting at church later in the day.

When she heard the buzzer, signaling the end of the washer cycle, she walked quickly into the laundry room to transfer the load to the dryer. As she raised the lid of the top loading machine, her world suddenly turned upside down. Violent dizziness seized her, and she bent over the machine, clutching at the edge of the exposed tub. The hinged lid fell on her head, with a sharp whack, and she lost her hold on the machine. She slid to the floor, her back leaning against the dryer, her legs straight out in front of her.

For an unknown length of time, Velma sat there drifting in and out of consciousness, and aware of pain in her back and legs. She tried to change her position, but discovered that one leg was crossed over the other, and would not move. She tried lifting her leg with her hands, but lacked the strength to accomplish the maneuver. She prayed. "If you are ready for me, Lord, I am ready to come home," but she continued to struggle to change her position.

33

The laundry room opened onto her bedroom. As she struggled and prayed, suddenly a large screen like a movie screen appeared before her eyes. It seemed to be in the bedroom at the foot of her bed, about eight feet from her helpless body on the floor. The image of a woman appeared on the screen. The woman did not speak, but Velma felt non-verbal communication urging her to once again try to move her legs. At last she was able to uncross her legs, and flexing one knee, eased herself forward to a half crawling position. From this location, she could not see the woman on the screen, but continued to feel encouragement and warmth from the bedroom.

Slowly and painfully, Velma half crawled, half rolled from the bedroom to the living room. Knowing that her purse was on a low chair, she was able to reach into it for the medication she knew would decrease the dizziness. She lay on the carpeted floor for some of the day, and finally pulled herself to a sofa where she could reach a phone. She could not remember how to call for help, but managed to answer when her son called at 4:30 p. m.

Within minutes, she was on the way to the hospital, and after two days of treatment, she was back in her apartment. Velma now wears a Life Line necklace. One touch brings the Rescue Squad, the police, and her family. "I had to wait ninety years to see my guardian angel," she joked, "but I always knew God had one for me."

Velma will celebrate her ninety-third birthday in 1999. She lives life to the fullest, continuing to serve her Master, her church and her family.

ANGEL
OR SAMARITAN?

An angel from heaven appeared to him and strengthened him. Luke 22:43 (NIV)

Drawing by Nikolas Bogdanovic Brinkley, Age 8

THE TRUCKER: ANGEL OR SAMARITAN?

Frances Brinkley Cowden

When the phone rang after midnight, as other mothers would, I prayed that was a wrong number. But on that late summer night the voice on the other end of the phone gave me the news I dreaded to hear.

"Mrs. Frances Cowden?"

"Yes. Wha-what is it?"

"Do you have a son named Clay Brinkley who drives a white van?"

"Yes, what happened--is he all right?"

I don't remember exactly what the next words were. But he spoke in a reassuring voice something like: "Do not be upset. Everything will be all right. But your son Clay did a flip-flop on I-40 near Hazen, Arkansas. He is being taken to Stuttgart Regional Medical Center. He is going to be okay, but I want to prepare you. His face has been split into three parts. But he looks worse than he is because he is so swollen. Just be careful and take your time getting here."

"His brothers?" I asked. Clay and his two brothers, Guy and Charles, had left that night going toward Little Rock, each one with a van loaded with tools that they peddled on the road. This was a summer job that paid for their college tuition and most of their expenses during the academic year.

"They are with him now. Don't worry."

The man told me exactly how to go to the hospital. He explained he was a truck driver and had seen the wreck and stopped to help. He had been behind the van when the accident happened. He described the accident on the CB, thus alerting Clay's brothers who were ahead of him on the highway. When they couldn't arouse Clay on the CB, they turned around and found that the wrecked van was indeed his.

I don't remember much about the hour's drive to the hospital. My husband drove, and we took the directions we were given. We found Clay just as the trucker had described.

I will never forget how my son looked when I saw him for the first time. His face was red and swollen three times its normal size. He had just been sewn up by the doctor. And as my messenger had told me, his whole face had been sectioned into three parts. The bone around one of his eyes was crushed and his nose broken. But he had no other broken bones and his eyesight was not destroyed.

Every one teased him about how lucky he was to have landed on his head.

When I heard the description of the accident, I wondered that he was alive at all. He had just put new tires on his van, but they were not strong enough to support his full load of tools. He had a blow-out on one tire, then the weight shifted and the two tires on the other side blew. His van flipped over and over spitting out tools, leaving a trail for several yards. The van was smashed like an aluminum soda can. The old van did not have seat belts and he was thrown out of the window and landed face first on the grassy median. He was extremely lucky not to have been hit in the head with the tools that were flying like bullets. We felt he probably would have been killed had he stayed within the van even a few more seconds. It was truly a miracle that he had lived!

When I tried to locate the trucker the next week to thank him for his help and concern I could not, although I had taken down his name and truck line.

Several years later I asked my son, "Clay, do you remember the man who helped you the night of the accident when you were almost killed?"

"You mean the one that saved my life?"

"How did he save your life?"

"He called the ambulance and then stayed with me until they came. He pulled the grass off my face and kept the mosquitoes fanned away."

"Do you think he was an angel?" I asked.

"Probably. At least he was someone God sent to take care of me."

How did the trucker give such good directions when he had not accompanied my son to the hospital? Who gave him my phone number? How did he call before my other sons did? Was he an angel or a very good Samaritan? Does it really make a difference?

SENT BY GOD

Rosemary Stephens

My husband I had been visiting his parents in New Jersey and were on our way home to Florida, when an unforgettable incident occurred in our lives.

I had fallen asleep in the car after lunch, and when I awoke, we were surrounded by whiteness. "Did it snow? Oh, it's cotton!" I exclaimed. Cotton fields as far as we could see to the right, left, behind us and in front of the car, lining the road, covering the entire earth. "We aren't on the main highway, are we?"

"This is a short cut," my husband said. "The cashier at the restaurant said it would take about thirty miles off our trip."

"It's lovely, but lonely," I observed.

"A couple of cars passed us before you woke up. This is a state road that cuts through some big cotton farms. Hey, what's that?" Our car swerved and we both heard a kind of clunking noise. Then the engine turned off as he guided the car over to the shoulder of the road. "Maybe we're out of gas," he said.

"We got gas before lunch," I pointed out. Surely our gas tank wasn't leaking. The car was only a couple of years old. My husband knew nothing about motors. He had never fooled about with cars the way my father and brother had done, for my husband had always had a good mechanic whom he trusted.

After raising the hood, he stared at the engine for a few minutes, then poked about with a stick for several more minutes. Shrugging, he checked the gas tank. Then, returning to the car window, he said, "I don't know what's wrong."

A car whizzed past us.

"Flag down the next car," I suggested. "They can send a mechanic from the nearest garage."

Twenty minutes later, there was a next car, and it too sailed by. Half an hour later, a car from the opposite direction also failed to stop. Then I noticed a house just beyond the field to our right. We could see a chimney and part of a roof. "Maybe they have a phone," I said.

"It would take at least an hour to walk there and back. I'd rather try to stop a car," he grumbled.

No cars. Then I cried, "Look! Something's coming!"

Moving toward us on the edge of the road was an old farm wagon pulled by a mule. As it got closer, we saw that the driver was a man wearing farm clothes. "Maybe he works around here," I said. "Or lives over there," my husband suggested. We had not even noticed the dirt road that cut through the field toward the distant house until the man turned the wagon into it. He stopped the mule and just sat there, looking at us.

"Thank God you're here," my husband called to him. "Do you know anything about motors? My car won't start. Is there a phone in that house? Can you give me a hand?"

The man said nothing. He seemed to be studying my husband, then our car, then me, for I was getting out of the car, pulling on my fur jacket against the cool air. Then the man looked up and down the road and across the vast fields.

At that moment his eyes locked with mine. My blood seemed to scream, "Danger!" He's going to rob us, I realized. But he flicked the mule with his whip and the wagon began to move onto the dirt road.

41

"Will you come back and help me?" my husband called. The man looked back at him, gave a quick nod, and the wagon went on.

"Nothing to worry about now," my husband said with relief. "If he has a phone, he'll call a garage. Anyway, he'll be back soon."

"What's the matter with you?" I said. "That man is not going to help anybody!"

"Nonsense, he'll be back, you'll see."

I said nothing. The wind grew colder and I returned to sit in the car. My husband stood beside it, watching the road. There were no more cars. After about an hour, he said, "Here he comes now. I told you."

Now there were two men in the wagon. As they came closer, I saw the guns. The second man was holding a long shotgun across his lap. The driver had placed another gun so it leaned against him, beside the seat.

I closed my eyes. "Oh, God, please help us!" I prayed silently.

"These are evil men -- I know it. Please help us. Send somebody, please. Don't let them kill us!"

I was trembling so badly I could not move. My eyes were open now. The wagon still had a bit of ground to cover before it would reach us. "Listen," I said, intending to warn my husband, but he was saying, "I knew he'd help us."

Just then something swerved around us and brakes squealed in front of our car. A tremendous truck materialized before our eyes. We had not heard it coming. It had a lot of very big tires beneath it, and it was hauling Texaco gasoline.

A very tall driver stepped down from the truck's cab. "You folks need some help?" he asked.

My husband told him what had happened, and the young man said, "Let me take a look."

42

"Oh, God, thank you, thank you!" I whispered. I was finally able to move, and I got out of the car. The wagon had stopped when the truck pulled over. I could see the faces of both men clearly now, and I was terrified. But I still clung to hope and trust in God.

The wagon driver dropped the reins and reached for his gun, but the other one grabbed his arm, and said something in a low growling voice.

"Thank you for your help!" I called. "But this man has everything under control. We appreciate your kindness, but we don't need your help any more. Thanks again."

Both men looked at me. Their bodies were like zombies, but their eyes were wary and chilling. They whispered to each other, then the driver turned the mule and they went slowly back through the cotton field. Halfway to the house, they stopped the wagon again, and sat there, looking back at us as if waiting for something.

I knew they were waiting for the truck driver to leave. When he can't fix it, he'll leave and they'll come back, I thought. I knew they would rob us, kill my husband, and, finally, murder me.

"Please, God, please," I repeated like a litany. "Please."

"That ought to do it," the young man told my husband. "Try it now."

The car started on the third try and I burst into tears. My husband offered to pay the trucker, but he refused with a smile.

"There are several gas stations this side of Raleigh," he said. "One of them is the station I service. They've got a good mechanic. Tell him Mike sent you. He'll fix your fan belt and replace the distributor."

I walked with him over to the cab of his truck. "Please do one last favor for us," I said. "Be sure we get the

43

car going on the road ahead of you so that you can see everything is all right. I'm afraid those two men might come back before we can really get away from here."

"Sure thing," he said.

So we finally left, with the big truck following us. After a bit, it passed us, the horn blasting away. We followed it for miles. Cotton fields gave way to trees, grass, houses, and stores. The road took a big turn and the truck disappeared from our sight. After we made the turn, the road straightened again.

"Where did he go?" my husband muttered.

"He just -- vanished," I said.

We looked carefully but there was no crossroad, and he had not parked in any of the driveways or store lots.

An hour later, we saw the Texaco station, and my husband pulled in.

When he finished talking to the mechanic, I told the man, "A Texaco driver named Mike told us to stop here. Do you know him?"

"Sure do," he grinned. "Great guy. He delivers gas here every Thursday. Nice fellow."

Today was Monday. I knew then that God had sent us a miracle. A guardian angel named Michael is in the Bible. Maybe a whole troop of angels are named Michael. Or did God pluck a very kind, ordinary man out of time just long enough to save our lives?

I've always believed he was really an angel, sent by God in answer to my prayer.

THE POSTMAN WHO CAME LATE

Martha McNatt

My daughter's voice on the phone was not normal. I knew something was wrong. "You may want to come over," she said. "We have just come home from the emergency room. Jeffrey was attacked by a vicious dog. His injuries are not permanent, but he needs to see his grandparents."

It was the day after Christmas. The temperature was in the seventy-degree range. All the neighborhood children were riding their new bikes and skate boards. Jeffrey, age eight, and Michael, age six, were in the middle of the throng. Their mother was also enjoying the late December heat wave, circling the neighborhood on her bike and stopping to visit friends along the way.

At one end of the cove, three puppies escaped their backyard fence and waddled into the midst of the bikes and boards. Jeffrey is an animal lover; fearing the puppies would be injured, he and two other children, (including his brother, Michael) left their bikes and attempted to lure the puppies back to safety in their own back yard.

Puppies and children were squealing noisily, while unnoticed in the yard across the street was a large Siberian Husky tied to a flimsy fence. The husky was barking and straining against his leash when suddenly the chain broke and the dog raced toward the children and puppies, teeth bared and bristles raised.

The two younger boys climbed to safety in a speed boat parked in the street, while Jeffrey headed for a

45

Magnolia tree with low hanging branches. He almost made it but the dog knocked him off his feet, and he fell on his back under the spreading limbs.

The child was helpless against the attacking animal. He covered his face with his arms as the dog bit and slashed into his upper arms and shoulders.

Michael abandoned his place of safety in the boat and raced toward the area where his mother was biking, but before anyone in the cove could reach the scene, a postman in a small mail vehicle came around the corner and became the hero of the day. He grabbed the dog by his collar, and pulled him away from the child, receiving a few slashes on his arm before the dog abandoned the fight and retreated to his own yard.

"He was a lucky little boy," was the comment we most often heard following the incident. We, his family, do not accept the word "lucky." We believe Jeffrey was saved by divine intervention.

The postman who rescued Jeffrey was not on his usual route. A last minute shift in scheduling sent him to a route to which he was unaccustomed, and he was more than an hour late. A chance happening? We do not think so. The postman was in the right place at the right time to rescue a little boy, whose jugular vein was the object of the dog's attack.

Jeffrey is now fifteen. His upper arm and shoulder scars are barely visible. He suffered no permanent psychological damage from the experience. I glimpse the scars often enough to remind me that he is our own personal example of the promise in Psalm 91:11.

A VOICE

Vicky L. Tignanelli

It was December 31, 1981, New Year's Eve, and a bitter, cold Pennsylvania winter was blowing. I was scantily clad for the disco and was accompanied by a new gentleman I'd met. He decided that he didn't want me smoking around his friends and he took my cigarettes from me. I got into one of those don't-even-try-to-tell-me-what-to-do moods and stormed out of the place. It was 32 degrees outside; the cab ride home would cost at least $40, and I was in that mood. So I started hitchhiking -- big mistake.

God did send his messengers, but I turned down each person's offer for a ride. I walked until I couldn't walk anymore; I was about an hour from home. I remember stopping along the highway to rest.

The next thing I knew, I was being pushed down in the front seat of a car. Blindfolded and gagged, I could hear young voices laughing, just two kids out for a joy ride. They took me to an abandoned farmhouse and repeatedly raped me. Every single orifice of my body was used. When they threw me out of their car, I was covered with urine, feces, semen and vomit. My rapists were two sick youngsters. But I was alive.

Then I heard the voice. The voice hadn't been there during the rape; it only spoke to me afterwards.

In a hushed tone, an almost inaudible whisper, the voice said, "I am with you."

I thought that perhaps I was delirious. After all, I had survived a most horrifying ordeal, and I was indeed

47

wounded both physically and psychologically. Maybe the voice wasn't really there. But I still listened.

I remember pulling myself to my feet, wrapping what was left of my black disco dress around my torso, and trying to avoid sleep. I would have surely frozen to death.

The place to which I was thrown was an overpass, a bridge on which a concrete abutment arose. I leaned against the cold stone and the voice said, "Do not sleep."

I remember not minding the voice, not being frightened or worried. I remember a great comfort and solace surrounded me like a cloud, like an electric blanket. Although my body must have been physically cold as it began to snow, my mind seemed warm, my senses tepid. I don't recall being able to see anything, but I could feel the snow on my cheeks and I could hear the voice telling me not to worry.

Exhausted and powerless, I finally succumbed to what the voice told me not to, and I fell asleep lying against the snowy, concrete wall.

Then I was touched. Touched by the most gentle of hands, by fingers void of bones or muscle; it was as if I were being lifted into mid air in some magician's show.

My bruised body would have felt any hand against it or any fingers that touched it, but I felt nothing. The wind against my face told me that someone was carrying me, but I felt absolutely nothing under my weight. It was as if I were floating.

As I was elevated, the voice speaking to me was serene and tranquil, with a sort of hypnotic rhythm.

"You'll be fine. You're going to be all right. You're with me now," it said, neither male nor female, simply a melodic, generic tone.

Next, I could distinguish automobile sounds: the motor purring, the smell of vinyl, the car heater's warm air.

But the hands that held me, or the arms that surrounded me, were like nothing I'd ever felt before. I could identify human voices whispering so that I could not hear them. But the voice that spoke to me was of a very different quality, so surreal, so undeniably God-like.

I could have died that night, yet I had been saved. I later found out that three nurses in a yellow Volkswagen Beetle were on their way to Atlantic City to watch the sunrise on New Year's morning. They apparently saw me lying in the road, picked me up and took me to the nearest hospital. Or did they?

I never found those nurses. And I really searched for them. The attending physician in the emergency room told me about the yellow Beetle and about them being nurses. When I tried to find them, I couldn't! It was like they had never existed. Nurses would have surely stayed with me during the hospital examination. Nurses would have given their names to the police. Nurses would have known that they were witnesses to my bruised and battered body. But there were neither reports by nurses, nor any names left at the desk.

The police and I later found the farmhouse where the crime took place. We discovered the spot where I was hurled from the perpetrators' car. We even located my earring in the place where I had apparently fallen asleep. But no one could track down those three nurses or their yellow Volkswagen. I never got to thank them, if in fact they did rescue me.

Today, I am a healthy and active 40-year-old. The rape will never leave my memory, that's what memories are for. But I do now believe that there were no nurses. Or perhaps those three nurses were angels disguised to walk among man on this earth. Whatever the real facts, I was saved by a voice and a pair of hands, the gentlest, calmest presence that I've ever felt.

49

I know I was touched by an angel. There is simply no doubt in my mind. And the angel waited until the strife and torment were over, after Satan had finished his work -- then my angel lifted me unto the hands of the Lord where I was safe once more.

NEED A LIFT?

Dean Cowden, as told to Frances Cowden

It was four o'clock in the morning, and I-55 in North Mississippi was deserted. Of all places to run out of gas! I could have sat there listening to the crickets until I went to sleep, but it was too hot with the windows closed and I didn't want to get eaten up by the mosquitoes. Surely an exit was no more than four or five miles. Well, I had walked farther.

I was cursing Guy, my stepson, because we had not stopped for gas sooner. The gas gauge wasn't working right in the company van, but Guy had insisted we had plenty of gas to get home from Atlanta--he drove the van all of the time. We had been exhibiting brass at a wholesale gift show in Atlanta for the past four or five days and we were really exhausted. I dropped him off at Nesbit, Mississippi, and planned to get gas at Goodman Road.

I had just gotten out of the van and started walking when an older model car drove up behind me. I could tell there was more than one person in the car; I tensed my muscles to be ready for whatever was to happen. It was too far to run back and lock myself in the van. I was afraid to look at the car, and afraid not to.

The noisy old car stopped beside me. An attractive African-American woman got out of the driver's side. She was dressed in work clothes, not evening clothes, so that was a good sign. But I still did not know who else was in the car.

"I saw your van, are you having trouble?"

What if they want to rob my van and need the

51

keys. This was the first thought that came to me. But then I felt a strange peace.

"I'm out of gas." I said, watching her carefully, afraid I had said the wrong thing, yet I trusted her.

"Come on," she said. "I'll take you to the station. Get in the back seat."

Well, I thought here goes.

I was shocked when I saw her other passengers. What was she doing out this late at night or this early in the morning with such young children? There was a baby in a car seat in front and a three-year-old in another car seat in the back. I could not believe my luck. Then I began to feel concern for her.

"Ma'm," I said as we started off in the old car. "Why did you stop for me? You have these babies in the car, and I could've killed all of you."

"The Lord takes care of us," she said. "I saw your company van and figured you were having trouble. So many people have been good to me; I try to help out when I can. I just trust in the Lord to take care of me."

"Well, I guess we are both lucky," I said. "But what are you doing out this time of night?"

"Oh, this is morning!" She laughed. "I have to be at work early and I'm taking my kids to the baby-sitter."

"But won't helping me make you late?"

"Don't worry about that!" she said.

Not only would she not take the money I offered her, but when I didn't have telephone change, she gave me a quarter to call my wife, staying with me until I completed the call.

Later, I could not remember her name or where she told me she worked. It was if all of the details that would have made it possible to find her and thank her were erased from my memory. Even if she wasn't a real angel, she was that morning--at least for me.

ABOUT THAT ANGEL

Willis Forrester

What a treat came in the mail today: your note with the book introduction and my statement to you that "I need an angel." Now, I will tell you more about why I made that request that night.

On July 11, I had been diagnosed with prostate cancer. While home for the high school reunion, I was trying to get surgery arranged to have the gland removed. At the reunion, I really didn't know just exactly what was in store for me. I was somewhat frightened by the prospect of having a radical prostatectomy and the accompanying difficulties, and I was reluctant to talk much about it then. After all, it was a high school reunion and that is supposed to be a time of fun and remembrance, isn't it?

On August 31, I had surgery here in Atlanta. The gland was removed, and all the tests have indicated there has been no spread of the cancer outside the gland. I feel that I have a new lease on life.

My angel came, not in the form of an individual, but in the form of the prayers and expressions of concern by my family and many friends, both here in Atlanta and elsewhere. I have been so deeply moved by these expressions and knowing that people were thinking of me, praying for me, encouraging me--all made the last few weeks much better. My angel has been all those people.

My oldest son John stayed with me a week during and after hospitalization; my neighbor cut the grass and brought food; friends have brought meals to my house; phone calls, get well cards, and electronic mail messages have come in a never-ending stream like floats in a parade.

I am so thankful for my angel.

You asked about my work. For 30 years, I worked with the Centers for Disease Control and Prevention--I worked in field assignments from 1965 through 1979 in Little Rock, St. Louis, and Hartford, Connecticut. In 1979 when I came to national headquarters in Atlanta, I worked in tuberculosis control and prevention, in refugee and immigrant health, and for the last five years, in the HIV/AIDS surveillance program. During my career, I was fortunate to work for a three-month period in a remote district in India (yes, I rode an elephant and searched for cases of smallpox in markets where there were real, live cobras in baskets with Indian men playing flutes to charm them) during the smallpox eradication program in 1975.

During the refugee and immigrant health work, I visited most of the countries in Southeast Asia, including a week in Ho Chi Minh City, Vietnam, in 1987, several countries in South America, South Asia, and Eastern Europe. Sometimes I would pinch myself to make sure that a lot of my experiences weren't just dreams, because after all, I was merely a farm boy from Whitton, Arkansas!

I retired from CDC in 1994, and took a position as Executive Director of the Council of State and Territorial Epidemiologists (CSTE) which is a professional association of public health people throughout the U.S., Canada and elsewhere. I directed the national office which is located here in Atlanta until I retired again this year. It was during a routine physical examination I was having at retirement time when the cancer was detected.

I realize that my life has been one of incredibly good fortune and luck, made possible I'm sure by the upbringing I had by my parents and by the experiences I had there as a child in Whitton.

Thank you for getting in touch with me and letting me share my angel with you.

A SPECIAL GIFT

Be strong and courageous. Do not be afraid...the Lord your God goes with you; he will never leave you nor forsake you.
Deuteronomy 31:6 (NIV)

Drawing by Madeline Colleen Brinkley, Age 7

ANGEL DEAREST

Blanche Boren

Yes, angels are real, they are not our imagination. They were created by God to help with his work in the world. I say to myself, "Careful, angel dearest is watching...."

My mother died during childbirth. I asked my grandmother with whom I was living many questions about my mother. She would hold me on her lap in her rocking chair and tell me things about Mother--what a wonderful person she was and how she loved and cared for my father, my sister and me.

As a child, I would question over and over again about why my mother died. When I was a little older, I asked again. My dear grandmother, holding me as close as she could, answered, "Some things we won't know the answers to until we get to Heaven and meet Jesus face to face. Your mother is now one of our heavenly Father's angels. Please believe that. Jesus loves you and will always love you and be with you and your mother will always love you too."

When I was twelve, Grandmother became very ill and we soon learned that she was going to die. As I sat on her bed for the last time, she held me close and said "My precious child, be strong, be happy. I will always love you. You will be fine. Always remember that Jesus loves you and will never leave or forsake you."

Afterwards, my sister Nell and I lived with my father and grandfather. Needless to say, I had to grow up fast; I had to help care for my sister and help do the housework. Even though my sister was a dear little girl most of the time, it was always hard for both of us. Throughout our childhood and even into the teenage years when times were really tough, I would remember what my grandmother said about Jesus always being with us, and to give praise to Him as we grew up.

Growing up without a mother was hard. Again and again I would remember what my grandmother had told me. Jesus would always be with me and never leave me and that my mother was one of his angels. I tried to picture her that way and would repeat the Bible verses, I Corinthians 13:11 and 12, knowing one day my eyes would be able to see and know the full extent of the attention that angels had given to us. I repeated these verses over and over as I prayed.

Time passed. I married and moved 750 miles away to Memphis, and within two and a half years was expecting my first child. My husband, Logan, and I both wanted this child. However, there was fear in my mind of dying and leaving my baby as my mother had left me. I prayed and prayed that God would allow me to have a healthy baby and live to raise him or her. I couldn't bear to think of my baby being left as we were left. I wished my mother could have been with me at this time in my life.

Three weeks before time to deliver my baby I became very sick with a high fever and the flu. The doctor put me in the hospital. I was very uncomfortable, depressed and sick. My doctor told my husband that he thought I had given up. This was not true. I wanted to have my baby more than anything, but I was fearful I might die and leave my baby without a mother, as mine had left me.

One night I asked God in my prayers why he took my mother when we needed her so very much. I was crying and praying and trying to remember what my grandmother had told me about Jesus never leaving me.

The hospital room was dark except for the light in the hallway just allowing me to see. I was still in my bed when all of a sudden my mother entered the room in the vision of an angel. She sat on the side of my bed and reached down and hugged me. She said, "I love you and have always loved you and Nell. You must get well. You have a big job to do to deliver your baby."

I told her I didn't think I could; I was too weak. In the most loving voice I have ever heard she said "Blanche, yes, you can. Tomorrow, you and your baby will be fine. Remember, I love you always and will see you again--'I can do all things through Christ which strengtheneth me.'" (Philippians 4:13) She hugged me and was gone.

She has never returned again; however, that visit from my dearest angel changed my thinking. I knew that if I ever needed her, I could call out. I believe God watches over me and that I will see my mother again someday. What a rejoicing day it will be! I pray I will make her proud.

My son, Richard, was born ten days later, a healthy eight pounds and four ounces blessing from God. I had lost the fear of dying. Three and a half years later, my beautiful baby girl, Kathy, was born. This time I knew God was in control and that my dearest angel and Jesus were watching over us. Yes, I do believe in angels, and I believe God's word when He says they watch over us.

Why are we fearful? Is it a lack of trust or of faith? Maybe it is both. In my walk with the Lord I have learned to trust Him more and believe that He did create angels to help with His work in the world. I think He knew that I needed to see my mother so He sent His angel in the form I needed to see.

A LOVING PRESENCE

Aloha Maxine Brown

The sidewalks were made of a special kind of cement in that part of the small town, which made them very smooth. Maxine, some of her cousins, and some of her friends, children of various ages, were gliding up and down laughing and shouting. Again, Maxine fell, but instead of bouncing up, she sat there staring into space.

"I have to leave and go back to Grandma's."

"Oh, don't go! We were just beginning to have fun!"

"No, my mother's calling me. Ma has died."

"How do you know? We're at least half a mile from their houses. That's crazy."

She was five, but common sense told her not to tell them about the silent voice inside that had started telling her things before anyone, including her, knew they had happened.

Ma, her great-grandmother, had been sick for about six months, and she knew that Ma was old. In her mother's big family, people died when they were old. Then everyone went to Littleton's Funeral Home and cried and finally, to the beautiful cemetery outside of town. Without her realizing it, Maxine had accepted the cycle of life.

At that moment, her cousin Robert who was six and a half came riding up to the children very fast on his bicycle.

"There you are, Maxine! Don't you know I've been riding all over town looking for you? Your mother has been calling for you. Ma died and your mother wants you back at Grandma's right now. Hop on the handlebars of my bike!"

Maxine hopped on Robert's handlebars, and Robert wobbled down the street until he got his balance. It was Maxine 's second mysterious experience that year. Still, she shared this knowledge with no one.

Ma's funeral left her with guilty feelings. She couldn't feel as sad as she thought she would. She and Ma had been rather fond of each other from the time she was two until Ma's illness began. She couldn't feel so sad because it was as if Ma wasn't really gone. She couldn't explain it, and she couldn't discuss it with anyone.

As she played or read a book, she would look around the room as if she expected to see someone. She felt a presence in the room.

"Mother, where do you go when you die?"

"To heaven or to hell."

"Does your body leave your grave?"

"No, your spirit leaves your body. All your relatives and friends are in heaven with you. You're always happy. No one is sick or poor."

"But suppose this 'spirit' isn't ready to go to heaven or hell and decides to stick around earth for a while? And what about angels?"

"Don't worry about any of that. Angels only appear to very special people. Why are you asking?"

"I just wondered."

Maxine had come to the conclusion that somehow, she didn't know how, Ma was there, watching over her in Ma's house. Was she upset because Maxine and Mother had moved there next to Grandma when Maxine was seven? No, the presence was warm and loving. Still, it was there! She was certain.

She had always had pleasant dreams in living technicolor and had slept well. She began to sleep fitfully, waking several times in the night and not remembering what she had dreamed.

One night she was especially disturbed, and she thought she had awakened. Moonlight flowed through the open window beside her bed. Mother was sleeping soundly in her bed across the room.

Maxine couldn't hear any sounds, though, like Mother's breathing or the usually noisy crickets. She leaned toward her window as she tried to hear a sound. Then, hearing nothing, she turned to the left of her bed. Ma stood beside her bed!

"Don't be afraid, Maxinie Honey! I won't hurt you. You've been so troubled that I am worried about you. Maybe I can help you."

"Am I dreaming, Ma?"

"Yes, that's the only way you could see me."

"Are you an angel?"

Ma chuckled in that little voice of hers. It and her expression told Maxine how much she was loved.

"Sort of. From now on, you'll be happy. I didn't want to leave while you were unhappy. I have to go now, but I'm not unhappy. You don't have to worry about me any more!"

Suddenly, it was morning and Maxine awoke rested. She was at peace all that day and all the days that she lived in Ma's little house. Ma was gone. She never returned.

Maxine never forgot the warmth of that loving presence in her childhood. With all her education, she could never explain it. At last, she just accepted it as a gift from God.

ANGEL IN PINK

Mattie Abbott

I spent my early life in a small Delta Community, not far from Memphis. I was the youngest of Mama's six children. Her first marriage produced four boys in rapid succession, and after ten years of widowhood, my brother Dan and I were from her second marriage. Our father was a wanderer. He was often away from home for months at the time, inspecting, buying, and selling timber.

Mama and the four big boys spent long hours on the farm from April to November, leaving Dan and me in the house alone, beginning when he was six and I was four. When Mama was in the house, she was always cooking. Three meals a day for four hard working young adults was a day's work, in addition to her farm chores. She had little time for her two younger children.

Dan and I were not resentful. We simply accepted the fact that the older boys were Mama's first concern. We became very close, and received with gratitude whatever tidbit of time Mama could give us.

I was delighted when at age six, I could walk to school with Dan. I fell in love with books, and made excellent grades, but I was often plagued with illnesses, and I sometimes missed as many days as I attended school.

As the years went on, Dan joined the farm work crew, leaving me to spend many hours alone. I became an excellent housekeeper, and I learned to cook, which gave me an opportunity to spend time with Mama.

A SPECIAL GIFT

The year I was in the eighth grade, I was struck down with rheumatic fever. I missed more than half of the school term, but I kept up my assignments, and passed the county-wide eighth grade test to earn credit for the year. My health improved during my high school years, and I developed a strong interest in the medical profession because of all the physical problems I had encountered. I wanted to be a nurse.

Mama wrote a letter to a relative who was a registered nurse in Memphis, and by the time I finished high school, I was offered a scholarship to the Methodist Hospital School of Nursing.

I had been to the city a few times, but the prospect of living there filled me with terror. I worried about my clothes. I had nothing pretty to wear. I began to dream of a pink dress. I made sketches of the dress I wanted Mama to sew for me. It would be soft pink, with rows of lace on the bodice and a pink ribbon sash. It would have bows trimming the short puffed sleeves, and a full skirt. With the pink dress, I would have white low-heeled shoes, and real silk hose.

No soft pink fabric was available in our rural general store. I had to be content with two drab cotton skirts and four blouses to begin my life in the big city.

A few days before I was to report to nursing school, Mama and I went to the general store and waited for the soft drink delivery truck. Mama agreed to pay the driver to give me a ride into Memphis and deliver me to the dormitory near the hospital where I was to live.

The time I had spent alone had not prepared me for the loneliness that settled over me as the truck pulled away from my home community. Mama and Dan were on the porch waving, but that gave me little comfort. The truck driver was kind, and made polite conversation, but my heart was heavy, and my hands were trembling.

I turned my face toward the window because I could feel the tears building. Suddenly, outside the window of the truck, an image appeared. It was a young woman about my age with long flowing hair. Thinking I was seeing a reflection, I glanced around the truck cab, but nobody was there but me and the driver. Neither of us fit the description of the image. In another moment, I knew she was not a reflection. She was wearing my dress--the one I had designed--soft pink with lace on the front, a ribbon sash and a full skirt.

She looked straight into my eyes and smiled. She continued to travel along beside the truck. She said nothing, did nothing, except float along with her long hair flying and the pink ribbon sash floating behind her.

By the time we reached my destination I was flooded with a wonderful sense of peace and security. When I stepped from the truck, I saw her no more, but the image is as clear today as it was fifty years ago. I have been able to invoke that same sense of peace throughout my life by recalling my angel encounter.

I have seen her only once since that day. A few years ago, I suffered a life threatening illness. In the hospital my heart stopped, and I was technically dead for a few minutes. As the life saving team worked to bring me back, I saw in my door, a momentary flash of pink and long flowing hair. In a few seconds, I was back and she was gone.

I have no doubt that the pink girl is my guardian angel. Her presence has strengthened my faith and enabled me to deal with a generous portion of life's troubles.

A MESSAGE FROM AN ANGEL

Geraldine Ketchum Crow

I awoke from a restless sleep dazed and confused. Beside my bed appeared an angel. Her head and wings were illuminated as she gently swayed back and forth. Then I moved about and felt the piercing pain tear down the center of my chest and radiate to both sides. That brought me to my senses.

Two metallic, helium-filled balloons, a gift from my granddaughter, were tied to a chair at the left of my bed. The round balloon's message was: "Get well soon." The heart-shaped balloon read: "You're the greatest." Air currents had eased the balloons together, one beneath the other, to form the shape of a winged angel. The room was dark, except for the glow of a small night-light, and in my confusion I thought I saw my guardian angel.

Slowly, my thoughts focused. Bypass surgery! The surgery that happens to someone else, but not to me. For three years the cardiologist had managed my heart blockages with medication. During that time I played the Pollyanna game fantasizing that somehow a new medical miracle would suddenly materialize, remove the blockages and correct my heart problems. But five days ago I was forced to face the truth. All of the available medications had been tried. Angioplasty would not work in my case. Bypass surgery was now my only alternative.

After the doctors had given this ultimatum I lay in silence thinking of the ordeal ahead. I had a history of allergies, severe side effects to medications and unusual reactions to anesthetics. What problems would this hypersensitivity cause? Too, I'd heard of others who experienced strokes after open heart surgery. Would that be my fate? If I should die, who would care for my aged mother and my husband? My mind and emotions were overloaded with questions and doubts.

Then I recalled a three-point plan presented thirty-five years ago by Mary Oler, a visiting speaker at a women's workshop. It was a simple plan, but in the past I had trouble keeping all three steps in operation for any length of time. I decided to try again.

One, DON'T PANIC. I seemed calm on the outside, but inwardly I wanted to flee the hospital, fly forty-five miles to our peaceful, quiet home in the country and never leave my comfortable surroundings.

That was foolish to contemplate for there was danger of a full-blown heart attack even while lying in my hospital bed. My responsibility was to relax and cooperate with the doctors and nurses.

Two, LOOK AROUND YOU AND HELP SOMEONE ELSE. Nine years ago my husband of thirty-four years had suffered two heart attacks. A year later my eighty-year-old mother endured a cardiac arrest. Both needed reassurance and a positive attitude about my surgery. Who better to give them that than I? For our two daughters and sons-in-law I could provide an example of faith and courage.

The three granddaughters were especially concerned about Nana. They had not lived long enough to know from past experiences the promises of God. "And we know that in all things God works for the good of those who love him, who have been called according to his purpose." (Romans 8:28, NIV). With God's help my surgery could assist in building this belief into their lives.

There was another group to consider--my family of friends, a family not by birth but by choice. And as I gave to both of these families, I found myself receiving far more from them than I gave. Thinking of others and expressing those thoughts took my mind off myself and aided in the healing process.

Three, and the most important, RELY ON GOD. I Peter 5:7 says, "Cast all your anxiety on Him because He cares for you" (NIV). During my five decades of joy and sorrow, sickness and health, success and failure I had learned the importance of trusting in God. Many times I had decided to turn everything in my life over to Him, but each time I found myself grabbing back this and that as if to say, "Move over, God. I'll handle this myself."

But now, what else could I do but place myself in God's hands? This time, because of my helplessness, it was much easier to let go and let God have full control.

This period in my life was not easy for me or for my family. Recuperation was slow and frustrating with some complications. In the hospital, angels of mercy in the form of nurses, doctors, family and friends cared for me and comforted me. Later, at home, God continued to work through His servants, my friends, who ministered to me with calls, visits, cards and letters, by running errands and by furnishing meals prepared by caring hands.

Sometimes my chest-centered scar shows its ugly head above a lower-cut blouse. I do not try to hide that man-made blemish on my skin; instead, I wear it with pride. Here is visible, positive evidence of how God, working through doctors, gave me a second lease on life.

It is now two years since that dreaded bypass, and I am well and happy. I am not particularly aware I have a heart -- the way it is with persons who have normal, healthy organs. My mended heart is filled with faith, love and gratitude to God, my family and my friends.

I often think of the angel at my bedside. Perhaps at that low ebb in my life I needed reassurance -- yes, reassurance from a balloon angel -- that God was with me and would never fail me. (See Hebrews 13:5)

GOING HOME

"The time came when the beggar died and the angels carried him to Abraham's side. The rich man also died and was buried. In hell where he was in torment, he looked up and saw Abraham far away, with Lazarus by his side." Luke 16:22-23 (NIV)

Drawing by Madeline Colleen Brinkley, Age 7

FAITH vs. THE DARK ANGEL

D. Beecher Smith, II

Not until I almost lost him did I realize how much I loved my twin brother. Although we were born identical, an accident shortly after birth damaged his eyesight, leaving his vision severely and permanently impaired, even with glasses. He never tried to drive an automobile but managed to get around quite well on a bicycle. After college he went to the West Coast, while I stayed in Memphis.

In Palo Alto, brother bicycled everywhere, placing himself at the mercy of some of the world's worst drivers, including one steering a gravel truck, not paying attention to the rights of bicyclers, who side-swiped brother and dragged him off his bicycle, and under the truck's rear axle.

That was when the Dark Angel came to claim him.

2

On a cool, mid-March Memphis morning the call came from Stanford General Hospital. The emergency room nurse's voice was sweet but sad, "Your brother's been in an accident. His condition's critical--the doctors say he has at best one chance in ten of living."

No! My mind screamed. Tears streamed down my cheeks as I clenched my teeth and vowed, "He'll beat those odds."

Whatever it took, organ transplants included, I was committed.

71

3

Have you ever heard that irksome noise inside the back of your head, where an insignificant word or phrase, or verse of bad poetry, or the lines from some dumb song like "Achy-Breaky Heart," kept playing like a broken record on a drugstore jukebox?

I'd visited an elderly Jewish client the night before the accident; she'd worn a charm bracelet bearing The Twelve Tribes of Israel, one of which I hadn't previously noticed--ASHER. As I spoke on the phone with the Stanford nurse, that old mental mechanism began, whispering repeatedly, inside my head, "Asher." At the time it meant nothing, but days then weeks of ASHER came and went, while brother's life hung in the balance.

Then came the setback: Sepsis--an infection in the blood that spread like God's curse in Exodus on the Egyptian firstborn, seeking to claim the elder twin. Dangerously high fever drove the doctors to say his time had come, and all the while the word "Asher" whispered away inside my head.

4

It was the Lenten season, when we Christians remember Jesus' passion, death, resurrection and sacrifice for us. For me and my family, our sole prayer was that my twin be spared. We repeated it constantly, over and over, individually and as a group. And, as we prayed, God listened. On Easter morning, the doctors declared the danger had passed. Brother would recover. Upon hearing the joyous news, the echoes of Asher went out of my mind.

5

My twin was moved to a private room with a telephone. We spoke on our birthday, the week after Easter. "You nearly died," I said. "What was it like? Was there a 'Tunnel of Light'? Did Grandma come to meet you?"

His already frail voice grew grim. "Nothing like that--different, dark, disturbing. I was in a twilight world. A Dark Angel had come for me.

"At first he looked human, almost beautiful, but with wings blacker than printer's ink. And, when I told him I chose Life, he changed: growing big and ugly, his hands became claws, cutting and tearing at my flesh. I tried to run, but whichever way I went he overtook me.

"Then I remembered it was almost Easter and I called upon God: 'Lord, deliver me, I beseech you, for You are everything, all-powerful, and I am nothing without Your strength. My soul belongs to You.'

"At that moment two Bright Angels appeared, bathed me in pure love, and delivered me from the Dark Angel. They came, they said, because I had chosen Life, and although I faced a difficult recovery, my prayers, and those of all who loved me, were being answered. It was God's will. Death held no dominion over me."

6

I'll never know what prompted me to ask the question, "What was the name of the Dark Angel?"

The phone nearly fell from my hand when my twin whispered the words, "Asshur..... Asshur-Baal. "

IMMANUEL

Walter Graham

I was at his side when Daddy left this world in September. It was a holy moment in which I experienced the presence of Immanuel -- God with us.

Daddy lay comatose in his own bedroom, struggling for each breath at the end of his battle with cancer. Mamma and I sat with him, each praying silently for the Lord to take him home.

I was in a dull stupor, staring at nothing, almost hypnotized by the constant whisper of the green oxygen tube under Daddy's nose and his labored breathing. Suddenly, I was aroused from my daze. I felt the distinct sensation of someone entering the room. I looked up, expecting to see somebody walking through the doorway, but saw no one. I thought: "An angel is here."

I had never seen an angel and wanted badly to see one. I saw nothing, but I was keenly aware of a very real presence that caused goose bumps to arise.

It was then that my mother's best friend, Sheila, came into the room, and I chuckled to myself, thinking "Sheila is the angel!" She and Mamma sang an old song to Daddy about heaven. I continued to experience the powerful sensation as they sang, and I searched intently, hoping to see the angel I now knew was with us.

Mamma and Sheila finished. As if he were waiting politely for their farewell song to end, Daddy breathed his last and was gone. The presence also departed.

Perhaps it was an angel. Perhaps it was Jesus. Whatever the presence was, it was real; and it was divine. God came for Daddy that day to take him home.

Today, December 14, is Daddy's birthday. During this Christmas season I will thank the Lord for Daddy. I will vividly recall my holy experience. I will smile; I will cry. But my tears will be tears of joy, hope, peace, and thanksgiving. I wish the same for you this Christmas: an encounter with Immanuel.

GOING HOME

As told by Helen Corbitt

Fred Snover was a Christian man, brought up in the Biblical tradition. He was a good Bible student and well loved by his many friends.

One night when coming out of the church at First Presbyterian in downtown Memphis where he attended, he fell and broke his leg. While the doctors had him in the hospital, they did some other surgical procedures which kept him in there for a month.

Before the accident Fred had lived alone in an upstairs apartment. Upon leaving the hospital, he went to stay with his sister, Helen. He was age 84 and never quite recovered from the other surgical procedures.

"One night about 8:30 he went to bed while I was cleaning up from supper. I went in to check on him and asked him if he needed anything.

"He was almost asleep, but he asked me, 'What are those two people doing in the room?'

"I answered, 'Honey, there is no one else in here but you and me.'

"He said, 'That's okay. My Redeemer hasn't come yet.'

"When I got ready for bed about 10:00, I went back to check on him again. He had gone to be with the Lord."

Drawing by Nikolas Bogdanovic Brinkley, Age 8

PILGRIMS COME TO LOURDES

An angel stirred the waters with her wing.
Our Lady, watching, standing on a knoll,
As pilgrims come for healing in the spring
And pray their souls and bodies be made whole.
They come on crutches...
In wheelchairs...
On stretchers...
Blind...
Devotion to Our Lady brings them here;
Their firm belief that she can cure them all.
These pilgrims here because so long ago
An angel stirred the waters with her wing.

--Patricia W. Smith

MENDING A PATCH OF HEAVEN

The jet, a silver needle,
Darned a denim sky.
Only men and angels
Can stitch a seam so high.

Russell H. Strauss

•§§•

SUNSET

God's chimneys flicker.
Stars and guardian angels
Report for night shift.

Russell H. Strauss

79

CONTRIBUTORS' NOTES

Mattie Abbott lives near Jackson, Tennessee.

Aloha Maxine Brown had her undergraduate and graduate training in theater at Bowling Green University in Ohio. She studied and performed professionally in Manhattan. Later, she taught high school English for 20 years and raised three children. Retired, she is currently a writer. In 1989, her adaptation of Hedda Gabler was published by Bantam Books in an anthology, *Six Major Tragedies*. Her poems, essays, short stories, plays, and articles have appeared across the United States and abroad.

Blanche Boren is author of *Thorns to Velvet: Devotionals from a Lifetime of Christian Experience,* Life Press, 1998. She is a member of Colonial Park United Methodist Church, Memphis, Tennessee, where she has served in various capacities over the years--Sunday School teacher, Bible teacher, church officer and United Methodist Women officer, a Methodist Hospital Auxiliary Volunteer and a member of the prayer group. Her first published stories appeared in *Our Golden Thread,* Life Press.

Nikolas Brinkley, and Madeline Brinkley, are grandchildren of Frances Brinkley Cowden and children of her son, Clay.

Helen Corbitt lives in Memphis, Tennessee, and is the only surviving sister of the late Fred Snover, a well-known Memphis photographer and poet.

Frances Brinkley Cowden is author of *Etchings Across the Moon,* South and West (1966); *View From a Mississippi River Cotton Sack,* GEC, (1993 and 1994); and co-author of *Of Butterflies and Unicorns,* GEC (1989, 1991, 1993 and 1994); *Our Golden Thread,* Life Press(1996). She is editor of *To Love a Whale,* GEC (1995); *Tennessee Voices,* The Poetry Society of Tennessee, and the *Grandmother Earth* series. A retired English and art teacher, she is founder of Life Press Writers Association. She and her husband Dean have 24 grandchildren between them.

Geraldine Ketchum Crow is author of *Bloom Where you are Transplanted,* Life Press (1996). She is a member of Chenal Valley Church of Christ, Little Rock, Arkansas. She has won numerous awards for her short stories. "A Message from an Angel," orginally appeared in *Our Golden Thread: Dealing with Grief through Faith,* Life Press, (1996).

Frances Darby, Memphis, Tennessee, is an editorial assistant for Grandmother Earth and Life Press. She is assistant director of Life Press Christian Writers' Conference. She had a poem in *Word of Mouth,* Poetry Today, Great Britain. She has articles in *Our Golden Thread,* and poetry in all of the *Grandmother Earth* series. She is the widow of the late Rev. James W. Darby, a United Methodist minister.

Valerie M. Esker is a self-described "late bloomer," although her love for the written word actually began at age four when learning to read. By the first grade she had won her first poetry competition. By her senior year of high school in Youngstown, Ohio, she had captured numerous awards regionally for her writing, and was featured as "Class Poet" in the Chaney High Yearbook. After her children were grown, she resumed her interest in poetry, entering and receiving awards in national contests. Now living in North Central Florida with husband Jim, publication credits include *Metaphors Literary Journal, Pig Iron Press, Poets Forum Magazine,* and *Just Poetry.* A retired nurse, she writes for the Beverly Hills, Florida, *Visitor.* She is a member of the National League of

American Pen Women, and is secretary for the Florida State Poets Association.

Willis Forrester was a classmate of Frances Cowden from first grade in Whitton, Arkansas, through their freshman year at Arkansas State University. They graduated from Wilson High School, Wilson, Arkansas. in 1957. See his letter, "About that Angel," for more information.

Walter Graham is an attorney and Executive Director for the United Network for Organ Sharing. He is a member of Huguenot United Methodist Church in Richmond, Virginia where he has taught the 36-week Disciple Bible study course for the past five years. He has authored devotional materials published in his church's publications as well as *The Upper Room* and has written several contemporary Christian songs.

Louise Stovall Hays had a story about her great-grandfather published by the *Commercial Appeal* (Memphis, Tennessee) when she was 10. Her writing continued in her business career: fashion productions and commentaries, speeches, promotional materials. Most recently she wrote articles for *Church News*, a monthly publication for the Episcopal Diocese of West Tennessee. Currently she serves on the Vestry and is a lector for Christ Church Episcopal. When she is not busy with other duties she is actively involved with the Poetry Society of Tennessee, The Memphis Art League and other organizations.

Gayle Hulsey was born in 1933, and spent her early life in the Mississippi Delta where she learned to love the earth, sky, wild life and all kinds of people. A Memphian for most of her life she went to "Ole Miss," Memphis State, and the Memphis Academy of Arts. Married for 45 years she has five children and 12 wonderful grandchildren. A realtor for over 30 years, she is now a member of MIFA Writers Forum, East Senior Citizens Center in Memphis.

82

Martha McNatt is a Christian writer living in Humboldt, Tennessee. She is a former teacher, and for fourteen years directed the Child Nutrition Program for Madison County Schools. She is the author of *Feeding the Flock*, a cookbook for church kitchens, published by Bethany House, and *A Heritage Revisited*, a commissioned work by First Christian Church, Jackson, Tennessee. Her work has appeared in each of the Grandmother Earth anthologies, in *Grandmother Earth's Healthy and Wise Cookbook*, and in Life Press's *Our Golden Thread*. Her hobbies are growing herbs, reading, watercolor painting, and Home and Garden, T.V. She and her husband Lynn are parents of two adult children, Terry McNatt of Germantown, and Linda McNatt Page of Jackson, who has just published her first book, *Quiet Moments for Teachers*, released by Servant Publishers, June, 1998. Martha is currently president of the Jackson Circle Branch of the National League of American Pen Women.

D. Beecher Smith, II is a widely published poet, writer and editor as well as a prominent Memphis, Tennessee, attorney. He is editor-in-chief and publisher of Hot Biscuits Productions. "Faith Vs. the Dark Angel," appeared originally in *Angel Whispers*. He is editor of *Monsters from Memphis* and *More Monsters from Memphis*.

Patricia W. Smith, Memphis, Tennessee, is editor of the *Grandmother Earth* Series. The poem which appeared in this collection is reprinted from *Grandmother Earth IV*. Very active in the Poetry Society of Tennessee, she is currently its president. She is also state president of the National League of American Pen Woman for Tennessee.

Russell H. Strauss, Memphis, Tennessee, is an officer of the Poetry Society of Tennessee and wins numerous awards. The poems included here were first-place winners and are reprinted from a *Tennessee Voices* anthology (PST, Memphis).

Dr. Rosemary Stephens, Memphis, Tennessee, is a widely published author of prose, poetry, and fiction. Her novels were published by Scholastic Books, her stories by *Seventeen* and literary journals. She has won national awards and has appeared in university quarterlies and anthologies. Her first collection of poems *Eve's Navel* won a publication award from South and West. She holds the Ph.D. in English from the University of Mississippi. She was first place winner of the Eve Braden Hatchett Tennessee Bicentennial Award given by *Grandmother Earth III.*

Vicky Tignanelli makes her home in Lancaster, Pennsylvania, with an African grey parrot named Coty. She is a medical transcriptionist and in her spare time writes poetry, short stories, and songs and designs crochet patterns.

OTHER LIFE PRESS PUBLICATIONS

Special prices may not apply unless ordered from the publisher. Add $1. 50 postage for one book plus $.50 each additional book. Mail order to Grandmother Earth and Life Press, P. O. Box 241986, Memphis, TN 38124.

Boren, Blanche S., *THORNS TO VELVET: Devotionals from a Lifetime of Christian Experience.* 1-884289-231, Blanche S. Boren, Kivar 7 cloth, 174 pages with 14 photographs. Uplifting look at life's experiences. 1998, $20.

Cowden, Frances Brinkley, *OUR GOLDEN THREAD: Dealing with Grief,* 1-884289-10-x, Ed. Contains personal testimonies and poetry of 40 contributors who deal with different kinds of grief using their personal faith. Kivar 7 cloth, gold imprint, 1996, $15.

Crow, Geraldine Ketchum, *BLOOM WHERE YOU ARE TRANSPLANTED*: Humorous and inspirational approach to moving from the city to the country. 1-884289-12-6 paper, 1996, $10.

Davis, Elaine Nunnally, *MOTHERS OF JESUS: FROM MATTHEW'S GENEALOGY,* 1-884289-05-3-- Biblical biography of the five women mentioned in Matthew. 344 pp. Perfect binding, 1994, $12. *EVE'S FRUIT,* 1-884289-11-8--Defense of Eve and implications for the modern woman. Perfect binding, 1995, $10.

GRANDMOTHER EARTH PUBLICATIONS

Abbott, Barbara, GRANDMOTHER *EARTH'S HEALTHY AND WISE COOKBOOK*, 1-884289-13-4 Healthy and easy cooking, but not diet. First layer of fat skimmed from Southern cooking. Optabind binding; $14.

Benedict, Burnette Bolin, *KINSHIP,* 1-884289-08-8 Lyrical poetry set in eastern Tennessee by Knoxville poet. Chapbook, 1995, $6.

Cowden, Frances Brinkley, *VIEW FROM A MISSISSIPPI RIVER COTTON SACK*--1-884289-03-7, Poetry, family values of farm life in Mississippi County, Arkansas. Cloth, gold imprint, 1993, $15.
TO LOVE A WHALE; 1-884289-O6-1. Learning about endangered animals from children and adults. Children's drawings, poetry and prose, Perfect bound, 1995, $10.00
BUTTERFLIES AND UNICORNS, ED 4, 1-884289-04-5 (Cowden and Hatchett) Poetry for the young and young-at-heart with notes on teaching creative writing. Perfect bound, 1994, $8.00

Daniel, Jack, *SOUTHERN RAILWAY: FROM STEVENSON TO MEMPHIS*--1-884289-17-7 1/2x11 with 400+ photographs, 360 pages, perfect bound, 1996. Signed and numbered upon request. Documents and other papers with heavy emphasis upon history of Southern Railway and its workers, $24.
MY RECOLLECTIONS OF CHEROKEE, ALABAMA, 1-884289-25-8, 1/2x11. 300+

photographs of author's family history and life in early Cherokee, 232 pages, perfect bound, 1998, $20.

Hatchett, Eve Braden, TAKE *TIME TO LAUGH: It's the Music of the Soul* 1-884289-00-2, Humorous poetry taking off on Eden theme. Chapbook, limited edition, 1993, $8.

Howard, Elizabeth, *ANEMONES*, 1-884289-27-4, Prize-winning poetry, all previously published, 1998, $8.95.

Schirz, Shirley Rounds, *ASHES TO OAK*, 1-884289-07-x Poetry of the lakes region by widely-published Wisconsin author, chapbook winner, 1995, $6.

SUBSCRIPTION OR DIRECT ORDERS ONLY:
$8 per year (otherwise $10 each)

1-884289-09-6, *GRANDMOTHER EARTH I*: 1995
1-884289-14-2, *GRANDMOTHER EARTH II*: 1996
1-884289-16-9, *GRANDMOTHER EARTH III*: 1997
1-884289-21-5, *GRANDMOTHER EARTH IV*: 1998
1-884289-24-X *GRANDMOTHER EARTH V: 1999*

INDEX OF AUTHORS